Cloud and Bone

poems by

Dale A. Lombardi

Finishing Line Press
Georgetown, Kentucky

Cloud and Bone

Publisher: Leah Huete de Maines
Editor: Christen Kincaid
Cover Art: Nancy P. Roberts-WHITE TREE
Author Photo: Dale A. Lombardi
Cover Design: Elizabeth Maines McCleavy

Order online: www.finishinglinepress.com
             also available on amazon.com

Author inquiries and mail orders:
Finishing Line Press
P. O. Box 1626
Georgetown, Kentucky 40324
U. S. A.

Table of Contents

PART II

for Kitty
who gave birth to me twice

for Kimberly
who first called me poet

for Steve and Katie
always

Don't turn your back on beauty
Climb into it, pull it tight around you
Steep yourself in it

until beauty becomes you
and you become beauty
and all that you bring forth is beauty

I

BULLSEYE

The poet takes the archer's
stance—feet firmly planted,
hips and shoulders in line
with the target, knees soft.

When her mind is centered,
she turns her head, grips
the bow, nocks the arrow,
locks eyes with the target.

With right arm patient
and steady, she slowly draws
the string straight back
toward her chin,

pulling, gathering
until the string has reached
its fullest expression.
She holds at that crest—

her breath
her bow
her arrow,
everything poised

at that steepest pitch
of longing
where every hope
starts to quiver,

where the hunted
quivers too,
bracing for what might be
its final rupture.

She holds, still—
then with a clean release
of fingers, sends a blur
of shaft and feathers

whooshing
toward the target.
Bullseye.
It hits gold.

The poet dissolves,
her body taking the slow
shape of a question mark
as she collapses to the ground,

the arrow she never saw
coming
lodged squarely
at the center of her heart.

ON A NIGHT SUCH AS THIS

Whether slivered or quartered
or full-to-beaming—even fuzzy,
when veiled by a curtain of cloud—
it is always there. And it is everything
I need on a night such as this—

when the branches of elm
are bent and bare, the fields
frozen under. A night when I wonder
how that sliver of sky-crystal can shine
its wordless light, make the snowscape

glow. How vapor and light, mingled,
can make their way from their place
in the heavens, down through the horizon
to sweep my anchored world with sky.
Then pass through my wintered window

to pour whole galaxies at my feet—
into a haloed pool of time itself,
deep and still, washed silver
with loves, losses, old stars.
Right here on my wooden floor.

NOT WHAT HE ASKED FOR

He asked for blueberry
but they gave him chocolate chip
by mistake

and by the time he took
the elevator up to the 7th floor,
walked down the corridor

to the last room, settled
into the chair by the window,
popped the lid off his coffee

and opened the wax bag,
he wasn't about to go back down
and change it. Instead

he pushed his glasses up
from the tip of his nose
and began digging through

the muffin, his fingers feeling
their way to every chocolate chip
he had not ordered

which he pinched out
then piled atop a paper napkin
on the windowsill

while the rest of us clustered
around her bed, wiping
our tears and saying

our I love yous and I'm sorrys
as the ventilator wheezed and rattled
and walked the last edge.

He sat apart from his wife
of 65 years with his head bent
low, continuing to pick out

each and every trace of chocolate
while his muffin crumbled
into bits around him.

He then closed his eyes,
brought the sweet remains
up to his nose

and drew in one long, deep breath—
hoping to smell blueberry
one last time

TUMBLEWEED

Imagine
taking the book of your life,
fanning out its pages,
then turning it upside down
and shaking loose all the words—
but not just the words—
what's in the margins
and between the lines, too—

Imagine watching them rise
on an updraft or scatter
to the ground entangling themselves
around that core question
at your center
as they skip and scuttle and spin
down the street like a tumbleweed—
gathering dust, gathering speed,
spreading seeds—

Will you have second thoughts
and run to grab hold
of some trailing truth or loose secret,
tugging and tugging 'til you set it free
to snap and sail on the wind
like a long silk scarf?
Will you wave goodbye?
Strain to hear
their giddy gasps of freedom
as they faraway fade?

And when at last you look back
at the book you're gripping
in your hands
and run your fingers once more
along its deckled edges,
what will you do
with all those empty pages,
unburdened now, nearly weightless,
like the lightly veined wings of a moth,
yet still so tightly bound?

DEAR NY TIMES FASHION EDITOR

I've just finished flipping through
the Women's Spring Fashion Issue,
your self-contained world
of feather hats, peep-toe shoes,
floaty fabrics and bloomers (*bloomers?*)

Page after page
of impeccable models
dressed in diaphanous silks
that billow and swirl
in the backdrop's impossible breeze

Pose after pose
of milk-skinned waifs
with vampy lips and vacant eyes
like holes to nowhere,
their flawless faces airbrushed

of urgency. Where's the invitation
in that beauty?
The heartbeat behind the mask?
Theirs is a beauty unpossessed,
evacuated—

and you can't clothe emptiness,
not *really.* Imagine if you'd let even
a spark of soul remain
in those now-deserted eyes
smudged with smoky shadow.

Just think if you'd left
those faces unslathered,
unshuttered—
Perhaps then you'd have ignited
in me a desire so desperate

for that snakeskin blouse
and organza skirt
(complete with crinoline)
that I could actually envision
my high-fashion self,

long-legged and strutting
down the boulevards of Paris
in those Prada stockings
and sequined heels.
Perhaps then you would have

connected with my soul,
unmasked as it is this Sunday morning,
and dressed (in case you're wondering)
in faded old jeans and a sweatshirt
baggy enough to hold my imagination.

RED-FOOTED TORTOISES DON'T DO IT

but baboons do
and lions do
and we do

if our brains need cooling
or we're bored or drowsy
or not particularly interested

in the fact that red-footed tortoises
don't do it. Just six seconds
it lasts—

long enough for someone nearby
to catch it—even your dog
if he's watching

Your eyes water,
your ears pop,
and whether or not you try

to stifle it, cover your mouth
with your hand, it still triumphs.
Just reading these words

can tip you over the edge.
So go ahead,
tilt your head back

take a deep inhalation,
give in to that familiar fullness
at the back of your throat

and let your mouth stretch
to its widest gape. Who cares
if anyone's watching?

LIGHTHEARTEDNESS

We have much
to learn
from a polka dot

HUNGRY

The teacups have all gone
quiet. Behind the cupboard
door, they hang in stillness
from their hooks

while they wait, hungry
for clattering and chattering,
for crook'd pinkies
and steeped secrets,

for deep conversation,
not just lip service.
Beside them, the plates
are neatly stacked—

the bottom ones
resentful of bearing
all the weight,
of always being shelved,

last-chosen, their patterns
still pristine, not chipped
or cracked or worn smooth
from use. They wait—

hungry for their flowers
to fade, for forks and faces
and for that hand,
hungry too, to open the door

to daylight and dreams,
possibility and purpose,
perhaps even the warmth
of an Eggplant Parmesan

IN WANT OF BLOOM

She's on the far side of beauty, having turned the corner on wrinkles years ago, but her pride is intact, and tonight she wears it like a breastplate as she dines alone at her corner table. She stares blankly at the air then glances down and slowly begins ironing a small circle of tablecloth with her fingers, ever so gently smoothing its tiny bumps and bulges. Her eyes are lost in the candle's flame when the waiter arrives and sets her dinner in front of her, reminding her that the plate is very hot to the touch. She nods and smiles (the faintest hint), unfolds her napkin to drape her lap, then lifts her fork and takes one measured bite, neatly blotting her mouth before taking another, as though the press of linen to lips could hold back her rising hunger, ages old but now newly aroused, in want of bloom—a hunger so wide and powerful and reckless that it flushes her face and threatens to burst the tight red dam of her lips and cry aloud. After her final bite, she holds the napkin to her mouth long and hard—sealing in desire, sealing out temptation—then sets it in a blushing crumple beside her plate. The waiter clears the table then offers the dessert menu. She shoos him away with a single wave of the back of her hand, then begins brushing crumbs off the table, neatly removing the last stubborn few with pinched fingers. She collects herself, straightening the new wrinkles in both tablecloth and armor. When all has been pressed flat again, she rests her hands in a tender right-over-left caress on the circle of warmth left by her plate. With softly sated eyes, she turns her gaze downward to the table, nods and smiles (the faintest hint), and this time, the table smiles back.

HARD-WORKING SKY

It is there, here, endless and ever,
a long way from home and yet not very far.
It flashes with fury and flutters with feathers,
holds raised angry fists and new falling snow.

It swallows horizons bruised purple with sunset,
clasps scrapers and steeples and spires and soot.
It hovers, hides, field-hunts for shadows,
is blanket, balm, a deep ache of blue.

It warms, swarms, warns sailors of storms,
cradles dawn as it breaks, catches night as it falls.
It shivers with twilight and oozes with fragrance,
the soft smell of sea spray, late grapes on the vine.

It rages and roils and slips through our fingers,
chases clouds and kites and wayward balloons.
It cups us and empties us daily.
Sometimes presses on us like a stone.

It carries the whispers of words left unspoken,
sings ages-old lullabies back to the moon.
It sweeps us along in tomorrow's direction,
sculpts the air with our dreams as it dares us to rise.

The sky holds our world
and our world holds the sky
in a rapturous rupture of time broken open,
a timeless reunion of first breaths and last,

of almosts and always, not yets and forevers,
of long ago roses and haloes of light.
The sky holds our place while it waits for us, too,
as we each dance our tiny steps here on its brink—

DRENCHED

Is it wind
or song
or field of tall grass
swept?

Hawk
or hush
or shadow
circling?

Rain
tears
or downpour
of memory?

OLD SORROWS

She wore a scarf
the color of old sorrows,
which perfectly matched her eyes,
and hung like unanswered prayers
around her neck. She stood

in her sensible shoes,
finally face to face
with that painting—the one
she'd heard about, read about
all her life—

the one that captured
the sunlight,
the brilliance of that day
in the south of France
some hundred years ago—

when the air was still
and the fields were afire with bloom
and the sun consumed the sky
and the whole sky was aflame
while the landscape blazed

beneath it.
Gone the shadows,
gone the contours,
but the *light*—
the *full yellow light*

burned and beat and danced
and leaped, and now she clutched
not her purse but her heart
as her heart poured out
and the sunlight poured in

and the flow between them
held—while they danced,
golden danced, her scarf atwirl,
her feet skimming the floor
in their pink ballet slippers.

FOR ALICE

away
wither
words
thoughts

self
entombed
shriveled
silent

alive
dead
both
neither

weep
she
can't
even

or
wail
so
why

do
I
hear
echoes?

CRADLED AGAIN

When I die
and leave behind

all shadow, pulse
and pearl

lay me on
a mute swan's wing

that I might glide
beyond this world

cradled on a hush,
drift to the farthest

edge of dream
cradled in downy prayer

then wingless, formless
catch the wind

rise into
moonless light

DRIFTWOOD DREAMS

I am moving through a dream
—or maybe—
a dream is moving through me

sucking, pulling
beyond the shallows
waters surging

splashing thrashing
sloshing turning
tossing churning

I keep dreaming the same dream
—but no—
it's different this time

swept to shore
far from home
breath of white mist clinging

battered beaten
stripped to bone
scoured sculpted

ghosted gray
twist of drift
broken into beauty

dreamed into being
redeemed
to be redreamed

FRESH INK

I read it in the newspaper
years ago

> A young family walking
> across the Golden Gate Bridge
> in the pedestrian lane
>
> the two-year old's hand
> clasped tightly in dad's—
> until
>
> her tiny hand slipped out
> tiny body slipped away
> slipped through a gap
>
> disappeared into fog
> into chop into churn
> into gone

Her unknown name was tattooed
on my heart that day

But even after all these decades
my tattoo has never healed

The ink still drips
The needles still pierce

MY BONES REMEMBER
I

I've started listening to stones—
those bones of the earth
from dark, from deep
that bucked and moaned
and heaved themselves
to the light

to be plowed aside, chiseled
and stacked, stone on stone
to guard their ground,
to stand beneath mist
and calling crow
while chipmunks burrow

and lichens glow frosted
under a million moons.
To bear wind and warmth
and pelting skies.
To bear witness.
And point the way home.

Even as every drift
of snow and melt
and every shift of land beneath
conspires to tumble, stumble,
scatter and crumble them
to humbled bits

I pick and pocket,
rub and turn—this way, that—
my fingers feeling their way
through dust and rattle
to long ago faces
and threadbare voices—

familiar, dear—
ground and horizon both—
calling me farther
into stretching fields
as weatherworn walls stand
guard my imagination,

and I
take the long way home.

MY BONES REMEMBER
II

I've started listening to stones—
to their pitch, their resonance,
their hearts thrumming
with messages, ancient and wise.

I listen for the pulsing
beneath their skin,
for the weight of their knowledge,
the knowledge of their weight.

I no longer hurry past
when I hear one calling
my name.   Instead, I stoop
down and turn my ear

to a weight even silence
cannot carry.
I mine for murmurs,
for mirrors,

that by listening,
I might see—
for I am like the stones,
I am made of clay

PREDICTABILITY

One morning when she
was three,
my daughter asked
Will we have
a night-time today?

At that startled moment,
I started thinking
how once our wonder years
have passed, we take it
for granted, this world of ours—

how it spins on its axis
turning day into night
and back into day again,
blue to black and back
to blue with no help from us.

It's comforting,
I might have told her,
that some things happen
with rhythm and regularity,
certitude even,

and that those things
won't change
in the blink of an eye
or when we least—

BRITTLE JANUARY SKY

with the wind
so tightly bound
that one stray gust
cracks it open

Crystal shards
rain down—
jagged memories
piercing with light

but not a light
that illumines,
more a bright
that blinds

broken glass
in my eyes
stained blue,
even the slenderest

slivers cutting deep,
till I bleed
warm days
and birdsong

CLOUDS, INTERRUPTED

Up here at cruising altitude,
the clouds speak their names

and shift their shapes
to tell their tales

of carefree sashays
across the sun, of tumbling

as ice crystals through high winds—
but not a wisp of protest,

not a drop of billowy blood
as this winged bullet pierces,

penetrates, assails them
with unsayable speed.

They don't surrender,
don't fall to the ground.

They simply soften their edges,
unfurl their sheared sorrow

and wrap swollen comfort
around the ruptured sky.

CONSIDER THE POMPOM

That fanciful fun-burst
sewn to the top of a hat
or onto the pointy tips
of Turkish velvet dancing slippers—

Oh, the pompom!
A most under-appreciated
embellishment, especially
in its most serious role

atop the shoes
of a stony-faced Greek soldier
dressed in his precisely
pleated (400 pleats) white skirt,

white shirt and embroidered vest.
Watch him as he marches
brawny and stiff-legged,
one arm outstretched,

its wide bell sleeve flaring
with purity of national purpose,
while the other arm slams
the butt end of his 11 pound rifle

into his shoulder with every step.
Each 7 pound cowhide shoe
is hand-stitched (300 stitches)
and hammered with nails (60)

to clatter on stone,
simulating the sound of battle
where there is none.
The silk pompoms at their curled tips

no longer offer toe protection
from snow and cold.
Their sole modern purpose
is to explode the gravity,

announce a readiness for fun
at the drop of a hat—or gun—
and kick tiny tufts of whimsy
into the all-too-serious air.

HOW WILL I KNOW?

Boil 10 minutes or until just before al dente

Will it be like that mysterious edge
between consciousness and sleep,
where one minute I'm trying
to tame tomorrow's to-do list
and the next, I've surrendered
to sweet slumber?

Or like that innocent moment
hours later, long after midnight,
when the first blush of day's light
softens the dark,
ushering in the promise
of shine and shadow again?

Then when that day,
and more days, pass,
and my heart and voice
have accumulated their bits
of gravel, at what point
will I cross that wrinkled line

into old age? And finally
at the far edge of waiting,
will there be those thousand suns
to warm me? A thousand faces bright
to light my way? Or just an inkling
twinkling at the verge?

> How will I know
> when it's *just before*
> it's too late?

BONES

When the weather
shifts

you feel it
in your bones

Cold
in the cracks

so cold
in the brittle

where marrow
once lived

Hollow bones now
like a sparrow's

but no air inside
for lift and trill

Just blinded ache
roaming the deep

haunting
its hundred homes

My heart aches too
when it's cold

But how—
when a heart

has
no bones

WHAT WE HOLD ONTO

we found him in the morning
his body a wreckage

he had left this life
ninety years and Parkinson's

the last earthly thing in his hand
what he held onto at the end

a flashlight

now it's my turn to hold it
because, he said

I'll need it to navigate the dark
I'll need it to navigate the dark

ATACAMA DESERT *
(ON EARTH AS IT IS IN THE HEAVENS)

after seeing Nostalgia for the Light, *a documentary about*
parallel searches in Chile's Atacama Desert: astronomers
scanning the heavens for cosmic origins and families sifting
the earth for remains of loved ones who "disappeared" under
Pinochet's regime

Here in this place—the only on our planet—
nothing is lost; everything remains.
Here, the air has never known
the weight of clouds, so night stars
shine on and on, unobscured.

And beneath those boundless glowing ghosts,
bones lie blanched of breath and blood
in their sandscape of secrets. Skies hold stones
and sands hold bones—graveyards, both—
nothing lost of white-hot centers.

And so, as if drawn by gravitational force,
ignited by desire for the clear, for their dear,
they come ... astronomers with their scopes
to study the sky and families with their shovels
and picks and weatherworn hands

to dig and sift, sift and dig
through unsayable horrors and long-buried hopes
for some trace of loved ones lost:
for the sparest of bones, the barest of bones,
for everything that remains.

They crawl, they claw, they pan for their gold
as bone-dry glitters of time and tears run
through their fingers. They spend their days
squatting close to the ground, sifting fistfuls
of sand while the transparent sun

beats them brown, beats them down
to breath and bone and desert desire—
dried husks of longing
that dig and sift till fall of night
when wind starts to whirl, joining

blankets of stars with blankets of bones,
swirling star dust and our dust
into one dazzling cemetery of light
as sand becomes sky becomes
stars become souls—

galaxies ablaze with dear ones,
clear ones, ones not forgotten.
And so enswirled in The Great Embrace,
they gather their tools
and turn homeward—

eyes burning, cheeks stinging
with scattered bits of stolen light—
tiny bits of mothers,
fathers, uncles,
fallen from the sky.

WHAT MIGHT BLOOM

if we transplant
the sky

plant not seeds
but stars

plant them deep,
set the whole earth aglitter?

II

"WHEN THE STUDENT IS READY
THE TEACHER APPEARS"

... flutter of feathers

student: Sing me, oh prophet and poet and pirate
      Sing me of rising on faraway winds

      Sing me of swooping unshackled to shadow
      Of piloting pathless through pillars of light

teacher: tu-a-wee tu-a-wee

student: But how can I learn to break free from my shadow?
      To untether my feet, so tied to the ground?

      How to unfurl and lift on my longing?
      Must I hollow my bones and fill them with air?

      And how do I hold all the light I must carry?
      Bow to the earth and rise even so?

teacher: tu-a-wee tu-a-wee

student: How to give voice to the blue-lit silence?
      How to thread meadows with pockets of song?

teacher: tu-a-wee tu-a-weeeeee

student: What do I do when my trill turns to tremble?
      How do I sing with this catch in my throat?

      Sing so hard that my vessel must burst?
      Sing so hard that there's blood on my breath?

      Sing so hard—

whoosh of wings ...

student: And how do I make such vastness home?
      How do I live both cloud and bone?

THE IMPORTANCE OF LADDERS

and I don't just mean
for apple picking or cleaning gutters
or painting ceilings—
I mean

the importance of all those ladders
that call to us, one rung creating
the need for the next
as we set our minds

on knowledge, thinking we might
be able to grasp a tiny bit of it
on our way to wisdom
if only we climb high enough.

I mean those ladders that steady us
as we set our eyes on beauty,
when nothing can stop us
from putting ourselves in its path

so we can brush up against beauty
as it sweeps across a riot
of rooftops or up-close breaks
into bloom.

I mean all those steps
of metal of wood of rope of air
that carry us up and out
of the layers

to that place beyond climbing,
that place beyond bird
or wind or cloud of thought,
that place where we are

no more from moon divided,
where we can shed our shoes
grown too small
and rest in the soft sling of time—

quiet but for distant ladders
falling, dark but for the light
from another deep
pouring from our eyes.

VIGIL

She finds her way back
to the place of the fallen

where old earth has reclaimed
young flesh, young skin

Naked bones remain
without their dreams

She scoops them
strokes them

smells the terror
feels the blind heat rising

feels the weight of her want
the want in her weight

the want to collapse
her own bones to a heap

what's left of love
more than her body can carry

She nudges, nuzzles
gathers branches and brush

covers hip, jaw, rib
then stands in silence

as old as that earth,
rocking her heft

from left to right
for endless suns,

her sorrowing trunk
weeping, sweeping

a hovering pall
of dust and dirt

while her grief-grey
elephant breath

mists
the grave

WHAT I KNOW AND DON'T

*the high tinkling trill of the winter wren

*the exact spot that causes a tickle

*why thick tears as the cello plays

*if everyone has a deep regret

*the French word for grapefruit

*why it takes so long for a feather to fall

*how silence does most of the talking

*my grandmother's last words

MORNING SONG

I need nothing
but these stone walls
along my path,
the morning misting
my face

My boots are laced up tight
and I do what I do—
walk to think
and walk to let go
of thinking

I give myself
to the rhythm
of steady footsteps
on cloudful earth,
to stars-turned-stone

that mark my way.
To trees, bent heavy
with night rain
and the field
not yet green

where a flock of geese
in black-necked rhythm
do what geese do—
peck peck away
the last stubs of winter

with every flash
of white cheeks.
Then there at the corner,
just beyond the tangle
of bramble—a daffodil,

abloom like my first face
freshly naked with hope,
does what a daffodil does—
sings—
without worry

for what or why
or how long the song,
or even if
anyone is listening,
it just sings

HOW TO BUILD A CATHEDRAL

Find a silent spot
Exalt it
Enclose the silence
with vaulted stone
Add some windows
arched skyward
to catch slants of light

Invite mystery in
Welcome a slight chill,
to be warmed by flames
of forgiveness
and the waxy scent
of deep, slow breaths

Layer in the fervor
of sweat-laden prayers
No need for pulpits
or pews or angels cast
in stone—just sweet
buttressed quiet,
swept clean

Sanctify the silence
so its hallowed hush
becomes a first-class relic
and people will travel
from far and away
to pass through

the heavy oak doors
and partake
so completely
of the stillness inside
that time disappears—
and later
when they emerge,

they are haloed
with quiet,
lit from within,
glowing grace
into the newly gentled
air

LOST WHITE

Like summer's envy of snowflakes,
Queen Anne's Lace covers
the fields—

I pluck one perfect flower,
gently brush its blossom free
of bugs, carry it home,

set it in a clear vase
of water, then add
a few drops of dye

and lean in close to watch
as red puffs and swirls,
then climbs and spreads

all the way up through the stem
to the dainty fretwork cap,
lost white now blushing

rosy, ruby, crimson.
We porous people are like that—
soaking up life's tints and taints—

and there's no going back
once scarlet begins to rise,
steeping us, staining us

burgundy, garnet, oxblood
before we spill over and infuse
the lives of others.

Sometimes we are dye.
Sometimes we are lace.
We are the well

that drinks from the well—
sometimes drowns
in the well.

BLUE

Upon a time once,
we lingered at night
as we gazed at the moon,
waiting to feel the bloom
of our own inner moons
and the slow ripening
of our dreams—

For what but dreams
and longing and wonder
ripen best by moonlight?
Sometimes I think we could survive
on moonlight alone—
moonrise, moonset,
evening-poured moonmilk.

But we've lost our night vision,
closed our windows to sky.
We bow our heads
to flash and flicker,
miss the welcome of ancients,
the parade of old stars.
But oh! we can click

and type in **moon**,
navigating our blinkered
brains and screens
with our fingers tap tapping
their way to that stilled familiar face,
now in its new compact size,
perfect for tucking into a pocket.

But the moon that rises
from the call of our fingers
is not made of old light.
It's not aglow with our dreams.
It's just a glow in our hands.
Or is it our dreams that have
dimmed and gone ghostly,

sleep-disturbingly
blue?

IMMERSION

I've lived long
beneath color-drained skies
and have finally learned
to speak *grey*—

but slowly, out of cadence,
as though my tongue
is broken. So hard to learn
this aching alphabet

with its dislocated consonants
and throbbing vowels.
So hard to master
the suck and stab

of sorrows on my tongue.
Perhaps I'll become fluent
once I begin to dream
in tones of bleak.

But now I still wake
from breezy blue
with a faint trace
of orange in my mouth

which dissolves
the instant I pull back
the curtains, see the sun
burning black

again

THE FLAVOR OF FUN

可口可乐
Coca Cola means "happiness in the mouth" in Chinese

Coca Cola: four tongue-cracking syllables
fizzing with fun, refreshing to the last *ahhhh*

Your mouth could be happy
with words alone—

Take for instance *bumblebee*
with its bursts and bounces and bumbles

Or why not try *calliope,*
feel it merry-go-round your mouth

Nibble on *chrysanthemum*
or edible *nasturtium*

Pair *pistachio* with *mustachio*
benevolent with *malevolent*

Namibian with *amphibian*
enemy with *anemone*

wiggle with *waddle* and *wobble* with *woozy*
wizard gizzard goblin floozy

flotsam jetsam riff and raff
rhino hippo uhoh giraffe

willy nilly flip and flop
topsy turvy tipsy—stop!

hocus pocus kit and caboodle
oompahpah and schnitzel with noodles

bibbity bobbity bolus and—
bolus??!

A *bolus* always comes along,
stops the sparkle, stops the song—

just a lump that sticks
in your mouth like a stone

GONE QUIET
I

Don't get me started.
I love them all—
Cow bells, dinner bells,
tiny tinkling cat bells—

So too the way my hand moves
across the page as I write
the word *bell*
in my cursive scrawl—

loop after loop
of swells and swoops
that nearly lift
right off the page.

Church bells,
wedding bells,
bygone goat bells—
especially those—

hanging from wide
leather collars fastened
with buckles of bone, etched
with time and a farmer's initials.

Think of the weight
of that dangle,
the clang of that jangle
with every bendy-kneed step,

setting goat ears to ringing
and turning their eyes square.
Think of the metallic taste
the air spoon-feeds back

into their bleating mouths
day after day
until that fateful hour
when the bell's clapper breaks,

untethering its tongue,
releasing that one song
for which it was made,
the broken ruin then tossed

into a forgotten corner
of the barn where it's abandoned
for years before making
its way to market

and finally to my wall,
where stilled it hangs,
the deep cave of its mouth
empty but for echoes

of wind and bleat and song.
Sometimes I take it down,
cup its dome to my ear
as I would a conch shell,

and listen—
for even stilled,
it sounds.
Stilled, it weeps

and trembles,
awaiting a firm hand
with an eager mallet,
for it too is made of longing

GONE QUIET
II

"Throughout their lives, the Paliyan tribe of south India speak very little. By the age of 40, they are silent. Those who continue to speak are considered abnormal, their behavior offensive."

Imagine spending your first forty years
trying to find your voice,
only then to return it
to the silence from which it came.

Imagine never again to ask or name.
Imagine giving up all the ways
you clothe what you want to say
with cloaks and veils and nets.

Imagine kicking down the verbal
scaffolds you'd spent your lifetime
constructing, so even the skeleton
of your tune is gone.

Think of your final words—
Would they hide in that hollow
at the back of your throat?
Hunch in a huddle behind your front teeth?

Would they roll around your mouth
like marbles or slowly melt away
like bitter pills—or sweet?
Would they be uttered

with stammer or stutter
or torn from your tongue
along with your name, your voice
given back to the voiceless?

Or would they be breathed back
to the air laced with song,
drifting like dreams out an open window,
blowing to some faraway elsewhere

where the whole sky rings
with the tinkling of a hundred
tiny bells tied to the feet
of a flock of pigeons in flight?

And once those last words
have moved through you,
your vocal cords gone slack,
would your tongue finally untie itself,

learn the value of stillness?
Or would it twitch
like a phantom limb
feeling for its voice?

And what would you become?
Breath or light or want or bone?

INTO ANOTHER WISDOM

Deep winter calls me
to ice-crusted fields

through a sleepy old gate
hanging loose from its hinges

opening and closing
with the wind

STARS IN OUR EYES

Pity the stars
adrift in the cold
for they know nothing
of their light or of the dark
that surrounds

and unlike the moon,
each has no face,
so when one dies,
who will grieve—
or even notice?

Pity the stars,
weary from shining,
never dimming or dividing
or withholding their glow,
never retreating

to the places where music
and poems are born.
Pity the stars
their wingless travel
through unimaginable dark

and distance, hurling
themselves light-years
through the heavens,
all the while weighed down
with our dreams hitched

securely to their contrails
as we try to ride
to their molten centers
and feel what it's like
for our cores to burn.

And yet ...

How to pity the stars
whose points of brilliance
still pulse with promise
long after they've died?
Whose reflections stay alive

in our heaven-turned eyes—
and whose dreams
stay alive, too—
for the stars dream
with stars in *our* eyes

FREE FALL

Stocks fall
Temperatures fall
Leaves fall
Snow falls
Niagara falls
Jokes fall
flat
Books fall
open
People fall
down, fall
back, fall
behind, fall
in line, fall
in love, fall
apart, fall
to pieces
Tears fall
Spirits fall
Skies don't fall
Shadows fall
Night falls
Words fall
short
Forests, fields
and we fall
silent, fall
asleep
Everything falls
away
Dreams rise

NIGHT BOUQUET

Some long summer evening
as the sky begins to melt
lavender, stay outside
awhile

Drift on the dusk
till your breath moves
free and true again
and the warp of night

enrobes you from within.
Let the soft scent of purple
guide you, pathless,
to that porous place,

those lush, wetted shores
where regret grows wild.
Go—
Gather up your lonely

and scared, full in flower.
Gather your blossoming
rasp and rage, your still-fragrant
blames and complains.

Part the long blades of guilt
to find even the tiniest
pinches of sulk and moan,
hiss and sneer.

Pluck them up.
And though your eyes
are misty now, search
for sprigs of self-pity.

Leave nothing ungathered—
the twisted and gnarly,
knobby roots,
clumps and shoots, all—

till your arms are laden
with a bountiful bouquet,
too large for any vase
but the perfect gift for yourself

once you twine it together
with forgiveness—yes—
and new hope.
Feel your heart beat clear,

then come to the peace
of deep purple turned inside out
as you carry your moonlit
bounty homeward,

vines trailing
through the velvet air

THE PRESS OF MEMORY

I like thinking
it will happen in November—
that month when the slow
yield of time gives way
to the press of memory,
leaves dancing their farewells,
the soft glow of candles
lighting the way home—

I like thinking
of shedding this husk
in a flourish of red and gold,
in a time of pumpkins
and firewood
and hay bales stacked
against the certainty
of coming snow

I like thinking
that this great ball of sun
will still anchor your days,
as stars will your nights,
and that the sapling
we planted that warm afternoon
will keep on rising
amid the songlines of sparrows

But mostly I like thinking
that rains will fall again
to soften the earth,
so when you visit me
　　(I can see you now—
　　hands in your pockets,
　　your collar turned up
　　against the chill)

you'll sink in,
come close again,
then carry a bit of me
with you back into your day,
the memoried mud
of my being
pressed deep and silent
in the treads of your boots

CHANGE OF HEART

Don't wear your heart
on your sleeve

*Make your face
your heart*

for then you will speak
with a single voice

Sing too
Your mouth will cry

your true pain
gasp your grief

Your unveiled eyes
will be window and mirror both

bright with vision
not just sight

and bright with flame
to light your loves

And when tears rise
as they will

your eyes will swim
in back-lit pools

of sorrows and joys
that don't forget

Others will have to turn
away, so true your face

Or will they be unable
to turn, so pure your voice?

And you?
Never again will have to turn

away from the sound
of your own voice

or the beat
of your own heart

THE CLEARING

Stop for a moment
as you walk among the ancients
and listen—*really* listen—

Beneath the creaks
and moans, you'll hear whispers
writhing, rising

telling what it means
to bear wounds, to bear witness,
to endure.

Find the one you know
by name, by heart,
and lay your hand

upon her wrinkled bark,
that crust that's survived
frost and scorch and sap run dry.

Read her fissures and furrows
like Braille, your fingers
feeling their way

to the break at her heart.
Look—*really* look—
at her crooked limbs

frozen in place, her skeletal
leaves now curled at their tips
with withered hope

and you'll understand
the pain of sameness—
spending day after day

under a fractured sky,
unnoticed and untouched.
Then look beyond

her gnarled limbs,
twisted trunk
and drooping crown

and you'll see beauty again
as you gently push her wheelchair
down cottony corridors

past doorways and dreams
and shades drawn at noon
all the way to that south-facing

window, where you can rest
in the clearing,
the things of the heart

not forgotten

IN THIS OLD WOMAN'S BODY

The changes have come slowly—

my face
now folds into itself
like an origami trick,
wrinkles ever deepening

my skin
has hardened to callous here,
thinned to paper there—
so too my heart

grey hairs
plucked away in my 30s
rinsed away in my 50s
now flare forth silver

my brain and voice
are more stumbling, less tumbling,
more pinched and bunched
and sprinkled with gravel

my eyes
have gone cloudy
but somehow
I see more clearly

and when I glimpse
my reflection,
I no longer ask
Who is this old woman?

but instead
What am I doing
in this old woman's body
when I'm just now being born?

ALMOST STILL LIFE

A nameless day,
midwinter afternoon,
this darkened room hedged
with quiet

On the table,
a vase of old water
holds a single aging tulip—
its stem gone slack,

petals splayed,
its once scarlet flower
now murky milky red—
faded grace at rest

as a slant of sunlight
slowly drifts toward it,
hovers then hunches
around it, steeping

it in a light so devoted
that the flower quivers,
straightens its stoop,
flares

becomes a vast field
of tulips,
becomes a thousand more.
How the light loves

the dark—so tenderly—
as it makes its unhurried
passage across the room,
and in the fade

of afternoon,
I'm left to wonder:
What does light leave
in its wake?

This day,
new eyes
that can see
in the dark

and ears tuned
to the sound
of a lone petal
falling

BREATHING ROOM

A poem must have
both cloud and bone—

room to roam roofless,
to billow and swirl

as through old abbey ruins
on mood-swollen moors

where a thousand breezes
blow 'round, blow through

my breath a cloud
'round columns and cloisters

through transepts and arches
of buttressed old stone

my thoughts a mist
through clerestory windows

blurring edges of sky
and longing and bone

till I become rock become
breath become air

and time is soft,
if at all

STILL I SEE YOU

In the years since you've passed,
I've gone blind—

Yet still I see you

        in the face of each old woman I meet—
        the *you* I will become

        in the face my glass gives back—
        the *me* who you were

And I see you most clearly at night
when I close my eyes and tip my face skyward—

the way a blind person sees the moon

JUST FOR THE RECORD

When I've reached that certain age
and you wonder about my mental fitness ...

    Don't ask me
    who's President
    or what year it is
    or even what month

    Ask me
    what finches are drawn
    to the thistle feeder
    or what color the fire
    when the hardenbergia blooms
    in March
    or how Willie-dog
    spent his final hours
    lying in the cool morning grass,
    face tipped toward heaven
    to receive the last
    of this earth's sunshine
    as a final blessing

    Don't ask me
    to count backwards
    by sevens
    or to draw you a clock
    or to tell you the time

    Ask me
    to tell you
    when time stood still
    or if I want more time
    or how time passed
    so quickly

Don't ask me
to take a deep breath
or to breathe normally

Ask me
what took my breath away
or when I knew beauty
so clear and pure and true
I couldn't catch my breath

Don't ask
to listen to my heart

Put your stethoscope away
and listen to what set my heart
on fire, what frayed
its very edges, or when
pride and awe and love
nearly broke my heart
open

Ask me
What really matters
Was it all worthwhile
Who I've loved
and how

Ask
What binds us to all eternity
What's at the very center
when all else is peeled away,
What will last—*really* last—
not anger or grief,
but music and art and poetry
and trees

Ask me
if I have hope,
not for myself
but for the world

And if I don't answer ...

Set down your hurry
Bring me a slice of calm
with some tea
Then pull your chair close,
take the pale wither
of my hand in yours,
and just sit, sit
with me
awhile

ACKNOWLEDGMENTS

I am hard-pressed to find adequate words to express the depth of my gratitude to all who have helped bring these poems into the world. But here's a try...

Special thanks to Bethany House and to the gifted poets and writers there who have given my heart a home. To my mentors, Kimberly Green, Kathleen Hirsch, and Steve Garnaas-Holmes, thank you for inspiring me at every turn. To Lorraine Cooley, Carol Copeland, Becky Evans, Greg Halsey, Wendy Haskell, Holly Humphreys, Jane Larson, Lolly MacMurray-Cooper, Daryl Mark, Bill Rich, Barbara Steele, Leah Waldron, and Peter Wenner, I am humbled and honored to write alongside each one of you. You make me not only a better writer but also a better person.

To the art of Poetry itself, thank you for making a nest in me, for transforming my heart and turning it towards beauty, *always* beauty ...
I will forever be your apprentice.

Tom LaGasse, it was my miraculous good fortune to meet you at the Hickory Stick Bookshop, jump right into soulful conversation and discover in you a most kindred spirit. Thank you for sharing your poems, for your deep reading and responses to my poems, for your encouragement, and your uncanny ability to point me in exactly the right direction at the right time. To Lynne Ackerman and Ellen Slocum, my early and always readers, thank you for championing these poems and for focusing your laser beams of attention and affection on me. It is in your light that I have grown more confident sharing my work. Lynne, thank you, too, for the most perfect line in this whole book: *an under-appreciated embellishment.* To Janyce Kittler, thank you for helping me trust, share, and steady my voice. I am deeply grateful for your insight, wisdom and clarity as I continue to learn how to live both cloud and bone. To Georgia Wostrel, thank you for cracking open my creative life by sharing your own. You are proof positive that a meaningful thirty-minute conversation can forge a heart-and-art connection for life. I remain ever humbled and awed at how you translated my *Night Bouquet* poem into stunning textile art.

To Jody Hetherington, thank you for your savvy editing and for teaching me about *too muchness.* To Nancy Pattison Roberts, my deep gratitude for your gaspingly beautiful *White Tree* that graces the cover. And to Leah Maines, Christen Kincaid, and all the staff at Finishing Line Press—thank you for bringing my first poems into the world.

To Barbara Daly, thank you for knowing my heart and sharing your own. Your deep insights and pitch-perfect humor inform both my process and my poems. Particular thanks, too, for gifting me with my first journal. It was in those blank pages that my first poems were born. To Kathy Farrell, thank you for infusing your close attention to my poems with a compassion, grace, and enthusiasm beyond measure. To Kathy Kurke, thank you for inspiring me with your stunning art and ever-engaging conversation. And most especially, thank you for always making me feel *worthy*. To Betsy McKenna, mon amie extraordinaire, merci beaucoup for the magic, music, and meaning you have brought to my life, and now to my poetry, ever since the first grade. To Jane Prinn, thank you for your generous attention and artful spirit and for companioning me every step of this new poetry path, from reading my poems to attending public readings and now to celebrating this publication.

To my brothers, extended family, and treasured friends who live at a distance yet encourage and support me from afar, thank you. I am grateful to each one of you for the many ways you have shaped my heart and turned it in the direction of poetry.

I have no words for my ever-growing gratitude to my mother, Kitty Anderson, but Rumi does:
A mountain keeps an echo deep inside itself. That's how I hold your voice.

And to my beloved family, Steve, Katie, Chris, Collin, Kyle, Lily Kate, and Dylan, this book is for you. It is you who add whole octaves to my life. You who have grown my heart. You who inspire and encourage and honor the poetry at my center. You who make me More. You who teach me as I watch you live large, pursuing your dreams and sharing your own gifts with the world. If hearts can explode with love and thanks, mine is now.

With growing gratitude and in loving memory of Peggy Murray, who I miss dearly,

Dale A. Lombardi

Dale A. Lombardi is a poet and conceptual artist who takes her inspiration from old trees, stone walls and daydreams in the Litchfield Hills of Connecticut. She had a poet's heart from the beginning, but the poet within lay dormant as she earned degrees from Duke University (BA) and Florida State University (MS), then juggled motherhood and careers as a speech pathologist, communication consultant and corporate trainer. Once she left the stress of careers and the vigilance of motherhood behind, she had space enough—and time—for the poet-artist within to emerge. Ever believing in the transformative power of beauty, she now spends her days walking, wondering, and creating.